SUGARTOWN

Other books by David Rivard

Bewitched Playground
Wise Poison
Torque

SUGARTOWN

David Rivard

Graywolf Press
Saint Paul, Minnesota

Publication of this volume is made possible in part by a grant provided by the
Minnesota State Arts Board, through an appropriation by the Minnesota State
Legislature; a grant from the Wells Fargo Foundation Minnesota; and a grant from
the National Endowment for the Arts, which believes that a great nation deserves
great art. Significant support has also been provided by the Bush Foundation;
Target and Mervyn's with support from the Target Foundation; the McKnight
Foundation; and other generous contributions from foundations, corporations, and
individuals. To these organizations and individuals we offer our heartfelt thanks.

Published by Graywolf Press
2402 University Avenue, Suite 203
Saint Paul, Minnesota 55114
All rights reserved.

www.graywolfpress.org

Published in the United States of America

ISBN 1-55597-435-X

2 4 6 8 9 7 5 3 1
First Graywolf Printing, 2006

Library of Congress Control Number: 2005925173

Cover design: Michaela Sullivan

Cover photographs: Aaron Siskind, *Pleasures and Terrors of Levitation 491* and
474, 1954, cat. # 181 and 180 from the series "Pleasures and Terrors of Levitation"
Art Institute of Chicago, gift of Dr. and Mrs. Irwin Siegel, 1992.799 and 1992.802.
Photography © The Art Institute of Chicago. Images © The Aaron Siskind
Foundation.

ACKNOWLEDGMENTS

Many thanks to the editors of the journals in which these poems have appeared:

The American Poetry Review: "Acceptance?" "After Borges,"
    "American Speaking," "Here Home Between," "Self-Portrait
    as a Boxful of Pigeons," "Sketch of History," "Stand-In,"
    "We Either Do or Don't, But the Problem Evolves Anyway,"
    "Wednesday in September"
CanWeHaveOurBallBack.com: "A Real Right Thing"
The Greensboro Review: "Delia," "288 Words for Rick Danko"
Gulf Coast Review: "Last Day of August"
Hunger Mountain: "But This Is My Face Now," "Self-Portrait as a
    Snowy Owl," "Schoolgirl," "Sugartown"
Memorius.com: "Thief"
Provincetown Arts: "Parents & Children"
SHADE 2004: "Delightful Soup," "To Danae"
Smartish Pace: "Soft Whistle," "Their Dreams"
TriQuarterly: " Asphalt, with Fading Dream of Quadratics," "One
    Darkening Mood Made Out of Three Months Intermittently
    Overheard," "The Benefit," "The Reverend Larry Love Is Dead"
The Canary: "You've Got to Remember You're Born"
webdelsol.com: "Self-Portrait as Anchored Sunlight"

Grateful thanks to the Guggenheim Foundation for a fellowship
during the writing of these poems.

Thanks, too, to these friends, for their support and more:
Stuart Dischell, Dean Young, Tom Sleigh, Steve Berg, Peter Richards,
Steven Cramer, Olena Kalytiak Davis, and David Daniel.

"Sketch of History" is for Ales Debeljak
"After Borges" is for Steve Orlen
"Asphalt, with Fading Dream of Quadratics" is for Gail and
    Michael Mazur

Tony Hoagland, Fred Marchant, and Michaela Sullivan all gave
clarifying responses to this book in manuscript—their insight and
love was sustaining.

CONTENTS

for David & Ginny Guenette

& in memory of Tom Sullivan

SUGARTOWN

AMERICAN SPEAKING

Pressure of what you'd hear
if you really heard
the findable pressures
of finite things—

you'd be concussed, actually,
by the carpenter
a Catalan or South Miami Cubano
60-something years old

and carrying a ladder
with inordinate care while complaining
in curses yelped
Spanish-style about the

hardening of his arteries,
his legs ready for the go-round
still, being on the make—
only, in this country

it's your money or your life,
and we don't want any
of those who slide into the pew these
Sunday summer mornings

to think the bedmaker
we call Jesus
has really died—after all, the sheets
so neatly & finally tucked-in

on all our beds
are clean, are they not?—so speak
American, says the crew boss,
speak American, OK?

and then shut the hell up.

HERE HOME BETWEEN

By the river—
out of which a white stag or inebriated
Pakistani taxi driver might step

to wet us down—
I have been given three distinct
not to mention

cloudless
dimensions to walk inside
the visible—

with a sparrow to my immediate right—
and the bird coptering

as it wishes
above a bread crumb almost

too big
for its beak;

      this sparrow being a clarification too,

it shivers there,
like a fat, blacklisted worker bee

the bird
hovers, inches above grass blades,

just ten feet
from a cat clued-in

but so benevolent
it chooses not to attack.

And that's it—
that's all—

this clarification was
absolutely all that it took:

      it's perfectly all right now,
      it's all right to soak through every surface
           and divvy-up the earnings—

how could it not be?—

there is this threshold
each of us must step across

if we wish to
stand before the crippled choirmaster

and sing.

ENEMIES OF ENORMITY

And thanks to a polymer the chemists jimmied-up in Bern
she can sweep a thin streak of blush across her cheeks
as any young woman might
if the spring is passing
as it is passing
through the well-advertised & transnational influence
of Chanel's "instant radiance to go"—
this skin of hers
a little skanky she almost thinks to herself
while staring in the mirror—
tho for this working girl & everyone else alive
today is a Tuesday a May 27th that no one can make behave
so that at the same time the girl is worrying her makeup
across the street in front of the post office
a panhandler in shorts is taking off his leg,
his plastic prosthesis unstrapped at the knee
its buckles bent & chafing, he holds his free hand cupped for coins
while the other rubs at the stump, absentmindedly stroking it
the way a man might the belly of his wife
if she were just three or four months pregnant,
that is to say, lightly,
his eyes inflected by worries, slight misgivings, fears,
but whose wouldn't be?
who wouldn't be afraid that the leg might be stolen?
it could happen, you might be distracted by a passing bus—
on the side of the bus a pin dropping in midair—
the pin imprinted there on the poster
the same pin
so often caught in the act of falling on a television screen
but in slow motion
as it bounces on a glass table

by the mouthpiece of a white telephone
clarity is what's at stake it's said, who we are—
a light tap when the pin hits the glass—
and even if no one is sure that what they've heard
is what they were supposed to hear,
exultant or glamorous, precarious or sad,
they will all go ahead with what they have planned
for themselves
if only
it could be a moment when they stand unburdened
before this evening's bloody meats
tomorrow's thunderclap.

THE BENEFIT

Outside snow on all
the bronzework & Georgian museum cornices, inside
professional white folk
under glass:

    suited bipolar disorders
    with compelling hairstyles & clout,
    being served by
    "people of color"—

Salmon Caviar & White Bean Salad
Ruby Venison Ragout
Bulgur Pilaf with Green Peppercorns
Creamy Fennel Purée
Mâche with Sautéed Pears

a suitable Volnay

and Maple Hazelnut Mousse—

    but over in the cortical warehouse
    of the jailer's tower, the
    county courthouse 11-stories tall

    three miles away
    in a dream one prisoner told of

    his loneliness, pointing to a hole in the snow
    there, the spot a bowlful of lentils

had been placed
sometime lately to cool.

Who knows what power really is? and force?
Which of us accepts that his life is real?

SCHOOL FOR MISCHIEVOUS WILLS

In the school for mischievous wills
a boy is dead tonight
dead of drugs & drunken dancing,
but at the rear of a backroad tenement
inside a new bulb
the tungsten wires burn,
a lamp hangs there above his bed,
a hundred-watt epicenter
in the midst of springtime pollen,
wide wide waves of dust
that the wind sends
skittering & eddying
through lamplight,
so that when the father
thinks of the boy
he thinks of him floating,
he thinks of a gospel boat & the boy
aboard it empty-bellied
but glad to be going
as the boat rides off at an angle
peripheral to the hillocks & docks
and the shabby wooden houses
from which he & all the other creatures
sinners & whatnot
have been lifted,
all those wandering out of so-called reach—
easier for the father to think of this
than of the god he prays to,
a Gulf Stream god with an appetite
for fantastic amounts
of both brown & white sugar,

a taskmaster,
he who requires of his dolphins
that they should ache
and be willing to be waylaid
for nearly next to nothing.

ACCEPTANCE?

"I am gone into the fields"—
just as it
was reported once
on a sign one

Percy Bysshe Shelley
saw posted
at Jane's cabin door—these fields,
as he then

knew them, breathing—
but getting there
is obstructed by getting there,
not by not

getting there—
and so there's this matter
of feeling oddly
small in the classroom

I enter today,
an adult
accompanying his girl
to school,

day after
the day after Labor Day.
Stretch out
long past who you are,

in either direction,
and, still, you come
swiftly to this
smallness, with its

new American
dictionary & aspiring
pencils carried seriously
in purple

and blue backpack,
its lunchbag
mayonnaise spotted,
joke book cracked,

and the corridor
long & having to be hurried down—
among the shy & the violent
this smallness

as quick on the
uptake as the shadow
of a pencil racing
its letters,

or fearful
at times of a possible
strangeness being
opened up

by wrong spellings
or faulty long division, those
inadequacies filled
with innuendo

and foreign bodies—
I don't know, now,
if any of us get out of this.
It doesn't seem likely.

ONE DARKENING MOOD MADE OUT OF THREE MONTHS INTERMITTENTLY OVERHEARD

February

A smell came over the street—lion-bright,
but sissified—somehow
it tasted of exotic antigens—so much so
that, for a moment, the clear sheets of shallow
rainwater trembled,
pooled where they were in hardpan
down at the construction site.

Two suits stood there talking.
It was all about Real Estate Re-Capitalization
and some up & comer they knew—

"I can't tell," the younger one said,

"I can't tell if Jack's
a poseur, or if he just doesn't know
what the fuck he's doing."

The smell had a professional heft, it was depressing.

How could we be brought so low?
just two days after our greatest national holiday,

the only one based solely
upon a rodent's shadow.

So much tasted of hatred then.

March

Waiting for the once-a-month
Magic Night at the Green Street Grill,

the drunk beside me
about to be shut down cold by the bartender—

stains on all ten of his fingers,
the oils
of a well-rubbed soul.

An enemy
with hobnail boots has rampaged
across his crocus.
Now it lies there,
smeared with dog shit,
way bent—

the great
improbable misery possible
of any life.

It must be opposed,

      tho sometimes it happens wrongly—
         like so—

"Give me another
sin & tonic," he says,
"I'm mellow."

April

False amnesty,

as when
early spring in the still cold mountains

the girls' choir having peed in snow & mud off-road
at sunset

they straggle back,
settling into their seats on a school bus named
Bluebird (tho as yellow as any other),

and because the bus driver
talking to a chaperone has said
"Wild turkeys are slim in the belly, not fat"

one girl imagines a flock, shot at,

two of the birds lying down like flushed cousins,
their heads entwined & touching,
blood still warm, coagulant
bloody feathers, ejected shells,

she imagines it,

then begins to forget, simply
by fiddling with her hair band—

an amnesty, a blessing,

"what a blessing is forgetting"

   —so they say.

WEDNESDAY IN SEPTEMBER

For so many of those
dead so recently
the air

must seem
a terrible substance
to be a part of—

actually having to be
carried
inside a baby's cry,

or worse
without choice having
to be threaded

all by oneself
through smoking wires
and mascaraed

lashes, through crinoline
and slurred words,
the spittle-drenched

but migratory words
of Ovid spouted
more or less day-to-day

beside the chitchat
of biophysicists
and knuckleheads—

the air is awful,
it's true, a companion
to vast

tensions, sad after-
effects, bewilderment,
and engine-drone,

and to breathe it
as we do
in the short run

we'd almost
have to feel that somewhere
very near

the edge
of at least one well-known
spring a sparrow

stands
as if tethered to a stone,
unable

to add even
a single feather
to the sky.

SELF-PORTRAIT AS A BOXFUL OF PIGEONS

They won't fly tonight, these pigeons,

    they won't take off in rain—

this bipolar wind & rain has blown away
all the noises that would have guided them,

all those barking dogs & grinding truck gears & church bells—

and so these pigeons won't leave—

    they won't go now until the wind dries out—

and of course that won't happen
until the express pulls in from Mexicali
and the moment arrives then for a striking porter
with a weak arm to throw a muddy brick
through a window three seats
in back of the beekeeper, the haughty widow
everyone likes to think of as our empress,
our royal scavenger of bee spit—

    and that just hasn't happened yet, has it?

the wind is wet yet,
the wind is wet

and the man who sleeps
beside these pigeons is so fearful
and so desperate
to know love

that in his dream
he has to stare hard at an anvil, sprawled
where he is on a sidewalk,
he has to lie there
trying to turn an anvil into a cloud
and the cloud into a woman
and the woman into rain—

   blond skinnyboned rain.

And in the cages by the man's head
the vulnerable & tired are asleep now too—

they're dreaming too—vexed birds,
the illiterate & beshitted messengers of the rolled-up
slipstream of days.

RIVER

Having survived for this long already
the deliverer of packages for FedEx
stands beside a river
happy now to have a cigarette in his hand
he wants only
to watch the greenish primavera of rapids in front of him
the daft swirl of water feeding itself
over rockspill the foamy garlands going screwy
because he would like nothing better he thinks
than to feel the lashes of his eyes
stirred by a fluttering wind
and he wants only to be apart
a portion of a small reserve
of warm sky & airwaves
and tho this driver
thinks hardly at all of being tired
as he stands here by the river
across the road
in the cottage of the town's kindergarten mistress
a television stops just long enough
in its channel surfing
to close-up on a flock of what at first seem to be
a hundred thousand owls
all of them with their ears missing—
a congenital defect, no doubt—
a savage shimmer
above the black letters that spell
the word SONY—
but they know what they want too, these owls
they know what they want
and so they are not owls

they are the fists of a crowd
full of purpose
and punching upward
in a floodlit stadium
where what rises above the cameras
is a single chant
"Death to the Great Satan."

THEIR DREAMS

The demands are everywhere fearsome in their dreams.

Someone to be the bride who burns down her church.
Someone to sail along the intracoastal waterway.
And another to beat the wasps' nests with chains.

"What's *Your* Problem?"
it asks on the heavily dented bumper
of the White Horse Taxi.

Death was named by those
whose cold cold grief could be comforted
only when they wore the frayed woolen sweaters
given them by their dead fathers.

ARMOR OF FEATHERS

Tangling forthwith
her fingers sticky from eating raisins
on the steps of the high school gym
a sunburnt swaying girl in denim short-shorts
kisses a crab-shouldered dropout
a hottie as they say, an eager sweatiness
a sleepy sly thought afloat there in his wrinkled black trench coat
a blood blister on the rim of his thumb
it's a real Jim Bridger that's buttoned tightly under his chin
and a Kangol cap of black leather
atop his head
the whiffle-cut bleached blond hair above his ears shining
no more & no less
than the tiny silver stud on the tip of her tongue
because the taste of raisins
in both their mouths
is planetary & pungent.

WE EITHER DO OR DON'T,
BUT THE PROBLEM EVOLVES ANYWAY

It isn't that hard, they say.

It doesn't amount to more than an ache, really.

Give yourself some space, they say—

as if the self were a cozy little back room, a small hall
strung with incandescent streamers,

and all that needed to be done, all that was ever required,
was to tear a few down.

But the problem is, friends,
        the problem is
there are a great many top-of-the-line things
that each & every one of us
has gone around saying we'd die for,

items of an apparently
absolute power
and perfection, in a variety of impenetrable styles—

"That's a color hair I'd die for," she says,
        speaking sometime in the afterglow of a dark haircut
            flickering by,

a bleak thing to say,

but so human, so sadly & completely full of the silliness
of wanting

that for once it sends
all the clarity suspended in the chlorinated sunlight
straight over the edge—

it haywires the clouds with lightning,
and the inscrutable sluices flood.

And what do you do then?

What do you do
when you've been set down
on the cool aluminum bleacher seats of the aquarium
and at the beginning of the sea lion show
you're asked point-blank
if you think it's true—
this thing you call acceptance—
and what would acceptance feel like
if you were one of those other children & adults
each & every one of whom
is a paraplegic
whose wheelchair has been parked
by the rim of the pool?

Because the sea lions are sleek things,
full of resistant veering powers.

And the wish to be given back
the child you were once won't work.

And the dominoes the laughing sisters
threw far across the grass
have been stolen now by rooks.

So don't speak too soon of acceptance.

That the sun stands apart
from all that it abuts,
unwilling to judge it,
may be our only real hope.

AFTER BORGES

If seen
objectively the cure might look
like this

this altogether
too bright day in late January,
the cold given over

to clarity
and all the facts gone temporarily
missing there

there, there it is
in a stoppered triangular bottle
on a crowded kitchen shelf

your daughter's
umbilical cord, cut off, dried out
saved

and what's ahead of you now?
bad breath
and mothballs the smell today

of winter woolens
in line at the Bread & Circus
checkout

the aging purchaser
of antioxidants
how vulnerable he seems

like a toothless cat
how nervous it is to be outside
avoiding poodles

fatty substances
frozen dog turds embedded
in snow & ice,

but near the basketball courts
there's a tree
a weeping cherry

leafless, blossomless
long whip-lengths of branches
a blank space

in winter remembering
gladly
a conversation there

with an Israeli
au pair or the aging Ukrainian
owner of a used-car dealership—

deities—
when sorrow lays us low
there are

innumerable deities
to turn to—for instance,
as it shakes the house's timber

that fire engine
traveling fast
down Inman, Engine Co. 9—

a Shinto belief
about the modest gods migrating
all over this earth.

THE REV. LARRY LOVE IS DEAD

He's dead now,

his balls will
never get itchy
again—
      because he's dead now forever—

his hair having been
hennaed free of charge
for one last time
by the Egyptian cosmetologists
at the Style Connection,
      there's no doubt now that he's dead—

Thanks to a fury
in his bloodhall,

he's good & gone forever.

The sun tho
is bright today,
      a constancy, a slivered glinting in the airstream—

and, musically speaking,
the blue jay
swinging amid our pines has got himself
a permanent hard-on
it seems—
      on the radio next door
the tunes of another era,
      still very much without error,

the Everlys,
the miscreant pheromone
Sly Stone, Barry White
of the undulant jherricurls,
and every 6th or 7th song
the always early-autumn river foam
of tenor Orbison—

    why does the world get in his way like this?

DELIA

The rain having been for three weeks
an on-again/off-again thing
on either side of this former toll road
where it rises to the Meeting Camp at Ezekiel Falls
and the sun being no better than a trumpet
tossed into far heavy grass
I would like you to know, Delia
O Delia! I would like you to know that
if you ever feel the urge
to misbehave or act out
in any of your old but currently forbidden ways
ways unbecoming of the evangelist pastor you have agreed to be
you should remember that day six years back
when you hied yourself to the mall
and from a small emporium
of digital shopware & entertainment systems
boosted an exceptionally lovely cell phone
the jellybean Nokia candy-clear kind
this one's faceplate violet, I believe
with a pushpad of Prozac-shaped buttons
remember how calm you felt after?
a shoplifter, but professional in outlook
you stood by yourself before the Newberry Records store
above you the poster of a singer with smile equally professional
on his head a hyacinth gray snap-brim fedora
bands of darker gray ribbing the crown
Frank Sinatra you thought, almost positive
—very like Sinatra, right?—
well, you were wrong of course
tho God forgave you this, & all else, later
he was watching you then at home

you were soaking in the tub, hair in a topknot, little breasts
shadow of a light blue vein near an aureole
your swarthy, pleasantly crossed thighs just below the water—
that was you, dear.

WISH LIFE, APACHE-STYLE

Oozy spring lawns & hip-switching walks—

and all the encodings
of the glandular having been
prioritized,

these come-ons
would appear to be subject
to roaming fees for sure,

       spoken as they are
       via cell phone—

"I can't give you that,"
she says,
       laughing,

this very toothy, very creamy Tinsley
           or Jen,

     red-haired & digitalized,

her lovely low voice & long long legs
in short skirt
a mischievous wave motion sprung brightly
across eyeball & tympanum,

"really," she
says, "don't even ask"—

a wave pattern—

a moment handed over
on a silver platter—

a series of flashes
telegraphed Apache-style
by hand mirror.

A REAL RIGHT THING

Like a green ludicrous tow truck
with yellow stripes & naked chrome bulldog
atop the hood, my pleasure's obvious
watchful wary arrogant & pure
the smell of warm December early the sixth
day the city men come to the park
to gather leaves half-disintegrated
already compost, that smell
there for the asking, those leaves
a few the color of her skin
at the end of summer, sweet present
blown against my lips—
                              Oh, that
was a good moment to be born in, serendipitous
for how the color set off her collarbone
like a silver belt buckle in a darkened church
and seeing her face then, so calm in sleep
I'll be in sympathy with a car alarm forever
so long as it never goes off again
and when I die finally it's certain the house flies
will love having this sick man around.

PARENTS & CHILDREN

Struck now—
        tho, let's face it, we're just
        adults
            stuck at a child's birthday party—struck by

laughter, & grateful now

    for the father
            (he who records the who & what
        of the birthday girl's gifts, for purpose
    solely of sending thank-you notes)   the father who says,

while pointing to a present being opened,

        "hey, look,
           it's a Victoria's Secret Barbie!"—

not true, but
sue me, it certainly sounds possible,

    well within the parameters of the American market,
    the memes & demographics, circa year 2000—

no, not a secret Barbie

    a "Victorian Doll," porcelain
    silk & feathers, rubied neckline, flat tum.

"That is not a toy,"

this clarification by Tehila
quite necessary—
                        what else?

a Madeleine Picnic Set
Audiotape of *The Lion, the Witch, and the Wardrobe*
            ("listen to this")
Magnetic Poetry for Kids, a kit
One ticket to "Arthur & Friends" the Wang Center,
            shakedown for a show Broadway-bound
Mousetrap ("a really complicated game," according to Amy)
and a Secret Code Bear—

            the thoughtful, caring generosity
        and savage expectations, the spendthrift
            sweetness of the kids here,

        Amir, Sara, Simone, Nina,
        Lily, William, Amy, & Olivia, here

for Simone's sixth birthday;

                        "Help me," Sara will say,
                later, wanting a Band-Aid,
        holding up a finger that won't be bleeding—

"help me"
the story often enough
arrived at,

            told, or not told—

"we look almost happy out in the sun," Tranströmer says,
"while we bleed to death from wounds we know nothing about."

> And that clouded spot
> on the windowpane
> is the oil & sweat
> left by the forehead
> of someone real.

DELIGHTFUL SOUP

Pulpwork & seed
in the sliced-open halves of
cantaloupe—
           it makes
of the weekend
a dank space
in which to be
bucktoothed & saddled
in the crossed-up
rain,
       this one
mood having fallen for
three days
on a tapping
aluminum ladder left misaligned
against aluminum
siding—
           but
let's face it,

after we have
scooped through orange to the green
of rind,

and the soup is on
and the sea boils,

at dark a woman
and man will swim themselves
stupid.

I know why—

     to be spellbound
     because their mother
     has died, & the two of them
     too poor to travel overland
     to her funeral,

tho what lie
wasn't she capable of
while alive?

You, you neighbors
of mine, I know
your business, you there

     basting in your
     angry juices,

but to be alive is to be
impatient,

and confronted by endless
questions any
mother is vulnerable.

If you need
to forgive, forgive her
now,

but don't
be dour about it;

      otherwise,
I'd rather spit
in this soup
than shake your hands.

SOFT WHISTLE

A soft whistle
pouring piccolo-style
through

empty space
along the river
a rodent wind

ruffling the water
inside Olmstead's cockeyed
little inlets.

It nudges the dock
belonging to the boat crew
from Alpha Chi

the weathered oak planks
on board which the gay *flambeur*
and blond BU coed

lie there sunning
and sweaty
the both of them

in spandex
black thongs by Jantzen
Swimwear;

and oiled-up (as
each is) each feels it
suddenly

as grave
and alone and
out of sorts

as a month of
Sundays bewildered
and cold

and couch-bound
in front of a festival of
spaghetti westerns

televised
by the A&E Channel—so surprised
it all seems

to matter so much more
than anyone
would have expected

SELF-PORTRAIT AS A BLIND SNOWY OWL

Some own it all
under the exclusivity of privilege,
the privilege of privilege a seemingly
infinite capacity not
to recognize itself
or so the story goes
until the Prince comes down
his jaw long & face shaven clean
his cheekbones high
and riding into the city
atop a filigreed royal chariot
Sakyamuni glimpses suffering then
he sees death & injustice
the naked toddlers at play in cesspits
the clusters of gaunt starving elders
menacing moneylenders, sullen slaves
he sees it all then,
and that changes everything,
that changes everything living
or seen by the living
into shared spaces
peopled with cares,
so that a quarter-century later
long past the hour
when he had first seen
how even kindness connects with fear
his path takes him
by the lawyer's sloe-eyed daughter,
she who as a result perhaps
of a series of small
shabby acts from third grade

to the nursing home
has been returned
as a blind snowy owl—
and when they talk
he describes to her
others he has met,
cutthroats returned as harbor seals
and nets full of gathered-up thorns reborn
as trim lawns
their sprinklers showering
the naked waistbands of demons,
after which she tells him
she's happy that she's blind, she's happy
she knows his brother's nickname is "Rabbit"
and she might have been obliged
to eat him
if she could see.

SCHOOLGIRL

Her hand, with its river girl rings
and its Gel-Pen

at breakfast crossing out
the eyes of Lincoln

>   (preoccupied as his
>   eyes so often seem, zealous, & without eyelids
>   burdened)

as they are here
on this rumpled
five-dollar bill,

>   his nerves hot, head troubled,

so that inking out his eyes
almost consciously it seems
her hand
has given him a sleepmask.

>   Sleep, you anxious liveliness!

On the table
that tin cup of milk waiting
to be drunk

will ensure
everything stays quiet, everything

except the accidental
September rain falling now
at such a mild slant

here in November Massachusetts.

STAND-IN

Let me sleep & then waken whenever life demands.
Let the dead baker of pies advise me—
he who was murdered by robbers
from a warrior clan gone bad—
his shift was long often but swift
his crust, the sugared slices of apples
stalks of rhubarb, all of it was quick
so if he says it is for the best
let me always be in touch with my loneliness
boots touching down on snow-covered paths
the clotted snow, sleet & ice like devil's snot
anxiety in the elementary school parking lot
a lot in darkness, tangle of
softnesses in darkness, the dark in darkness
that crow queen appearing endlessly
beside a bank of violet crocuses.
Let her always be watching me from her position
by the geriatric center—
at all times worn wild
in her affection for my shyness.
Let me mingle my feathers with hers
let my breath stir against her beak, snockered.
Elsewise I would be as pleased
to be a jar of baby food if having been eaten from & cleaned
it were filled then by the sea.

ASPHALT, WITH FADING DREAM
OF QUADRATICS

Day of creeping cars rain-flogged—

        and on this side street
where slag-trucks were idling yesterday,
     and morose Italians
shouting, those pavers & rakers

      being the instigators of fresh asphalt

       now there is a black spell—

it has been cast upon the old, scraped-up tarmac
and waits to be inspected by the city's
      supervisor of civil projects,
          the son of a former mayor, a stutterer.

     The black spell lies there—
        its beauty

       better by far

than that of our bright
     house reflected back
       nippled
by moonlight.

       It's stronger, & more toxic—

a chemical shadow the eye
                    wants to fly into,
as if it had caught a glimpse of

        what?
    a place the soul might hide?
someplace it could rest & be alone?

I couldn't say.
        And what exactly is the soul?—

            especially when the supereminent rain
slows, & the noise cuts out—

            now it's a light twang
        from elsewhere, some birdsong

in this lovely wet breeze, a creaking backdoor,
                out of which
a black police sergeant is hurrying in a green raincoat,
        a color last seen in the last of last night's

    dreams, a Benedryl-induced dream—

the rim of one of the wheelchair's wheels
        had been completely coated by a phosphorescent moss,

but the missing math homework
            Algebra II's quadratic formula
        was just about to be found.

288 WORDS FOR RICK DANKO

Oh, you can be made glad
that's good, meeting cheek to cheek
on a cold street, me too
but you should get yourself a warmer coat, for god's sake
a sloppy cobalt greatcoat
if it's the one a stranger wore once
by our last surviving elm;
meeting like this, our eyebrows are entangled
being caught out now like
the tips of narcissus, they're premature in the creaking January cold
snapping back
after a thaw, they're brave—
highly stupid too—
but brave
mostly, mostly
clever enough in the heavy falling mist
to be silent, it's good
good, let's be quiet
all over the playground, there's the phantom flash of kids
on the jungle gym, the Russian girls
with their amazing upper-body strength, so blond
and their mortal parents
bouncing, bouncing
bouncing on the balls of awfully cold feet
inappropriate footwear, nice
Mary Janes, loafers with soles as thin as fish bellies
but what could be better?
to be reborn an almost anthemic swallow?
one of those infinite celebrities?
or to be as something
otherwise

such as one of those candled eggs the world
wants warmed, or a high pile of coal
a hill in the shape of a graph
one of the fuels of the future
a melting bronze bell, or maybe fresh juice?—
air cargo is bringing green tea with triple echinacea—
but what's needed is a sign,
something that will make the choosing clearer.
That's it, over there
on the sidewalk, by the mailbox, stiffened pine needles
a Christmas tree dry
as a daddybone
chewed on
by a pit bull, it's nice
it's good we're meeting
so calm down, rest—
it's alright, your singing—
you, you're the one who's being
applauded now
by that blind black woman.

THIEF

That
you have to act as if you'd
broken-in—

what's that mean
exactly?

and the mist?
what can the mist
possibly mean

if it means one
thing to the scratch tickets

and another
to rose petals—they turn,
flower petals

turn, torn-up
lottery tickets turn,
in the wind

a steady stream
across
the sidewalk,

turning, the brick
sidewalk

sailing a little,
before settling
under

the same sky
boot heels
walk below—

but what does that
bring to the mix?

You're just a thief now,
come in
from a white squall of rain—

highway rain—

no one whose name
the headlines might out.

You're not unique.

I've let down those I love too.

I've swiveled around
and in the frozen cloud
seen the fire

all cross-grained
by rain. I've smelled the sweat
and perfume

on the wet towels
she left behind, & I've made a mess of
my name at dusk.

I was being called at dusk.

I can explain only this.

SUGARTOWN

Sweet & lowdown,

you do
have a tongue
on you tho,

and it's nice, what it's doing
        what it's done too
to that popsicle stick
    it's licking.

        But what it said earlier,
            it hurt,

I can't remember the words
    exactly,
        but they hurt,
    and had
on the undercasing of their circuitry
            the phrase
            "patent pending"
stamped in dark blue ink.

        You hurt all manner of beings alive,
        without knowing,

    as a wind would
descending out of storm cloud
            like a bejeweled hand
        to swat & rip

all the
bunting hung on the brownstone
City Hall—

it was tacked-up
by Mr. Jesseaume the janitor

in this part of the world

where his mother thinks she's dying
but wants to wait for one more moment now
by a yellow kitchen chair.

SELF-PORTRAIT AS ANCHORED SUNLIGHT

In every boat made of blue
balsa sent downriver with the wind for luck
a New Year's message.

I'll have no truck with that.

On the floor, stretching out
my arms warm in sunlight, spine straight, feet splayed
I lie like an anchor—

    it has a certain appeal,

        this being.

Possessing the clarity
of the formerly blinded now
will save me

from becoming one
of those things I have always wished
never to become—

    the skates of a weeping nun
    or the sails on any leaking triple-masted slave-runner
    fast or slow, the algebraic for the average pinworm's motility
    a railroad crossing in the middle of nowhere
    ditto any cheap plastic pulley
    or unfair tribal migration—

better take
this, this incidental
pleasure.

Won't return to it, ever.

TO DANAE

"Danae, in the promiscuities
of springtime I wish we

were as two zonked Ophelias
again—girls on Kawasakis—

having doffed our woolens
parents & perspective,

we would ride on scooters
risen out of bogland

sweaterless, with or without
nipple-rings, our lips chapped,

in great gravity our thoughts
forgotten two seconds

after thinking, only
would you not

let your mood resemble
so much the phonetics

of your name, Danae?
in denial you make us

into two ants devoted
to moving a bowling ball,

but in acceptance a hybrid
glance would pass

between us, electrons
shifting orbit, parted mouths

the portals of many words,
happy, histocompatible, smooth.

In this way, tooling around,
no clap of stoned lightning

would strike us, no
sea kelp cold & lunar

could wash out the road
at Hixbridge Crossing,

no wind harm us, please
discard your sadness,

as you were taught by
the child you were,

who once refused forever
to eat tail of ox

soup or shellfish—
in those days the ecstasy

of your enemies
was weak, much weaker

than yours,
remember?"

BUT THIS IS MY FACE NOW

But this is
my face now the hairs
of my beard my eyes
my mouth—

it speaks now doesn't it?—
at the end
of a warm September—
Here it is

it comes as
a sharer comes tenderly
to the spaces
a cicada inhabits—

it hovers shakily between
the sea foam
and the customs shed—
and tho it vanishes

sometimes
even if it does
I can reappear a little while later
simply by looking

and after that
my white moth too is freed
and fluttering as it were
out of a rogue state

and away from a scrapbook
stuck with glue
sooner or later it heads
toward sunrise—

Look at that light
pouring now
around his blue shirt look
at this man—

With his wild red birthmark
he stands there
instructing all of these mudflats
so calmly.

SELF-PORTRAIT AS *CONVERSO*

I might have been nameless
for years
someone lurking by the doors of an orphanage
his birth certificate soon to be sent out—
a secret moment in a wider world—
but as it was September
and as the asters were everywhere,
each of them having been wired
to a jolt of Daddy-won't-you-pick-me-up,
all I had to do then—
since I had been traveling for such a long long while by that point—
all I had to do
was to stand there shifting from foot to foot
in a shoe-repair store
while that black-banged
and malevolent idiot
the cobbler to whom I had taken my boots
sat at his workbench
and nattered on & on about the *conversos,*
those Sephardim who rode the Atlantic crossing
from Spain to Vera Cruz in leaking transports, *marranos,*
some of whom, upon anchoring at the Azores for well water,
had disembarked from their caravelles
to marry-in among the teenage daughters
of Catholic whalers & olive growers—
skinny-boned girls from Terceira, São Miguel, Ponta Delgada—
mist-calibrating & intuitive girls
like my mother & sisters—
and since I had already convinced myself
that it was impossible for anyone
other than the chosen

to have ears as finely tuned as mine
when he looked up & spoke
I believed what the cobbler said then—
"So yeah," he said, "yeah,
so, probably you're a Jew, right? probably, right?
Of course you are."

ENGINE ROOM

What if the aging bureaucrat a department-head
in mossy gray tweed sports-coat, red & gold rep tie
and button-down blue Oxford
his receding afro gray-freaked & tightly clipped
what if he sits alone
on a park bench across the street
tapping the fingers of his left hand
on the so-called bottom-line
the Center for Tobacco Control's 2005 Budget unstable in his lap
while the blood-orange oriole
machine-embroidered onto his baseball cap
watches or appears to watch at any rate
a green fly folding & unfolding its languorously iridescent wings
right there on the brim
that's the way it looks
this close to a man's thoughts
as soon as they have been provided with a nickname
the nickname he'd assumed so eagerly
during those years in the engine room
but to become another person
how could that be possible
while the destroyer sailed in humid coastal waters
he remembers he gave blood once
to save a blond gunner's mate
a Kansan who spoke of daddy's girls
curfewed girls & muddy hymnals
he liked to tell of choirs singing for rain
whenever the devil's hand mirror appeared in the sky
two hours later he was dead
there on the boat where it mattered most

that you wake up breathing hard & fast
when the order was given
"Come here," says a voice in the distance
a woman in blue culottes & halter top swiveling near a tot lot
"I'm serious," she says to a crying toddler
"Come here now."

LAST DAY OF AUGUST

As that servant
at the center of the universal itself
would have put it
all sounds
provoke questions
and have to do so insistently
the longer
they have traveled through space
tho whether it is hazy or not
is beside the point
the man thinks to himself
remembering his mother
and the walk they went on once—
the fatherless boy
is what he was,
his father having left
long enough before
that he might have asked
who his father was then
if he hadn't asked who it was
who sent the song there
that Beatles single they'd heard
come again now
to the air around his house
a sound among the planet's sounds
tilting far & wide
as if on a wavelength
all the way from Sarawak,
these questions being
asked being asked
out of a wish to live

as wholeheartedly
as anyone does
whenever a train rushes past,
the steel wheels melting a penny
someone laid atop the tracks
the face of serenely fated Lincoln
stretched in several
different directions
at once then
and at once always the point
at which a man must ask himself
again & again
whose blood is this?
whose blood is mine?
even tho to the flowers his mother
carried in her hand,
the goldenrod & Queen Anne's lace,
it's almost certain that these questions
would have meant
nothing
nothing at all.

YOU'VE GOT TO REMEMBER YOU'RE BORN

"Give me another
sin & tonic," the drunk says.

So much wind
outside then so much
wind every rascally human face
is like a balled-up
caterpillar rolling
atop a jinxed pale palm.

Right;—

but to the north
in the still cold mountains at sunset, that's
where the girls are
from the girls' choir—

having peed in snow & mud off-road,

they straggle back
to their seats now aboard the bus,
past a blond whose
red parka makes
the dim light ring,

while she sits,
wondering—her umbilical cord—
just what was it
her parents did with it that morning
it fell off?

SKETCH OF HISTORY

In the calendared world
opening all too rapidly now to sadness
it happens that
when these wars
we have witnessed so much of
for such a long inevitable time
all of a sudden
come to a halt
out of nowhere then
something sinless
and tightly freckled
appears—
in the twilight of a hexed suburb
a young girl's handstand
rises above a dry lawn,
a lily is found
atop a flower cart
in an old cow barn long ago converted
to coffin manufactory,
and operating well within the innuendo
cast by a 60-watt bulb
the lifetime of which is 750 hours in length
at lunch
the casketmaker who finds this lily
carries it home
to his wife.
It is at such moments
that each of us is capable
even if only briefly
of standing alone
but not at all lonely

inside our portion of sunlight,
an allowance
the entire wavelength
penetrates—
part of the wave inside us
part of the wave outside
as when in the corridor of sand
where lowland & ocean meet
and along which
we walk at present
the breeze is still & filled with afterlife,
the smell of the moment
Noxzema Marlboros Coppertone,
it carries
with it a commotion
from the other side
of the bay,
the splash of smashed concrete
and rusted iron beams, rebar
refuse & salvage.

YOU

If to breathe
means never to leave home
and never to return,

    then proceed—

without shame,
    or caution—

      breathe.

The sun will shine
all day along a length of
anchor chain,

    and any creature
    would be happy

      any rat beetle or caryatid
      who climbed the hawsers

would be delighted
to be aboard such a fast-moving
supercargo as yours.

It all depends upon

    you, my whole life

depends upon you.

DAVID RIVARD is the author of three other books of poetry: *Bewitched Playground* (2000); *Wise Poison* (1996), which won the James Laughlin Award of The Academy of American Poets and was a finalist for the *Los Angeles Times* Book Award; and *Torque* (1988). His work has won awards from the Guggenheim Foundation, the National Endowment for the Arts, the Massachusetts Arts Council, the Howard Foundation, the Fine Arts Work Center in Provincetown, and the Pushcart Prize. He teaches at Tufts University and in the MFA in Writing Program at Vermont College.

This book was designed by Rachel Holscher, set in Clifford by Prism Publishing Center, and manufactured by Bang Printing on acid-free paper.